heaved from the earth

new york 1971

besmilr brigham

Heaved
from the
Earth

alfred a. knopf

Some of these poems were first
published in *The Ninth Circle,*
University of Tampa Poetry Review,
South Florida Poetry Journal,
Ann Arbor Review, Camel's Coming,
Extensions, descant, ARX, Foxfire, Apple.

to roy and to heloise

Compiled under a 1970 fellowship grant
from the National Endowment for the Arts

Contents

Poems of Cold

poems
of warmth

The Fire-Ring
Poem

to live at last upon an island

in the middle of a river, the river
breaks
just before us its opening out to make
a way circling the still woods'
beaches, where

there is no real quiet. the current
raises with the sea
washed inward, and rushes
pouring down upon the flat areas
drained from the mountains, passes;
black wings

lift from the peaks, the wings
circle near
never come above us though we can
see them; through the breaks
close as a breath they come to us
then waver and turn back

always the wings have turned from us
big black angels in the sky
the rovers
though they will come—
neither river nor bird
are things we waited expectant for, sure
they close our circumference

for warmth
we build a small fire, poles and
sticks; it is not a fire one can see far
we cannot see it from the mountain
the river
hides it
even from either side of the lifting banks
yet we will work only each day
for pleasure of the fire

for warmth of the fire
on windy nights it throws sparks up high
and the smoke
circling against the cut-back tree limbs
from our brief shelter there
makes a sudden time of beauty
the animals
will sit away from us and look at
the fire

and we will only come out
for the supplies we need

The Green Tree

the sky is like the sea

in which claw and wing
great fish
swim the currents

the sky surrounds us
floats of watery air where
great wings
   windheld waves of sound
swing with the currents

wash over our straight postures
the land
stands straight up out of the sea
the mountains
look like islands in the sky

where strange birds
hoof and hand
hold fast, a wandering drove

moved with the currents

The Eagle

symbol, engraved on a coin
his struck image
against the blue held light
morning—
wings in air, the white under cloud
plumage
mixed with the storm of his breast

crying
   a black shaken thrown-rock soaring
head intent
before the dive

making his house of sticks and leaves
moss-fungi
the tremendous wings spread
motionless,
as the mountains

In the Month
of the Jaguar
# of Sweet Laughter

the whale and the little fishes were made
.   .   .
he hides the young in his mouth

the blue cat, scale-less

fish
the red blood-smears
shower before a delicacy of fin
floating link
                          bathing in
mud, the slither dance of water
his sense in time a refraction
from light
deflects upon his wide
rounded eyes, lens
wet sight our perpendicular bodies
green as trees, monstrous in
the air

a globe of hunting color as
he feels the earth

delicate as a willow branch
his sensuous flesh of skin
bucks the currents
he sifts
through streams the loose net-rays of
sun (shallows, and sleeps
half waking
high in the reflectant branches of leaves
root burrows
        hide his still form
flying wings, he sails through cloud-shape

Caught
in the Car's Lights,
the white owl

wings
before the racing wind-
shield
glass, through glass
we see it

white with the lights
against the snow

edges of the road,
seemed to be travelling with us
in speed
the under-place feathers

death
death of the bird, a point
                of lifting
awareness
against the white fields
the woods,
flying for wood-
line

The Marsupial
Opossum

from her slit pouch
tiny kangaroo babies
that hang by the tail

run with shadows against
a warm moon
they play in rays of leaves

   builds her nest
with rolls of knotted fungus-mold
her sleeping den

her body is a cradle
ears bare in snow
she hunts
the claw-touch feet
        in a white world

Your
Hands

measuring the tree's stalk
cutting off limbs
to pull
the blown scrawny peach

back to its place in earth
putting down
tight posts against the new
sweet-gum sprouts

to make a tree, some year
years from now the storm
forgotten
a boy will shake down
big gold plums, the purpling
globes
fall on a ground
where your rough feet walked

a hand
touch in the heavy fig growth, garden
where one
so without knowledge
learned

War
of the Ants

house of the coffee woods, bordering sun-
willows the great white flowering
rows of gardenias, river bank
covered in red blooms. migrating ant
burrows

the marching ants
crossed from island flows, the curving
swells
of their relentless lines and lines of
growth. we sat in the woods from them

after, when their slow sightless shapes
pressed over our walls, the big knotted
plant roots
               men from the town came
they poured gasoline into all the ant cities
escape holes, every entrance
carrying water to pour down draining
the passageways

and struck them with fire
the booms
ran under the ground with fumes and
moisture, like a giant below-in-earth with cracks
of lightning
that passed, that we could not see
for days
singed workers crept to the light
their red bruised bodies
pushing before them carrying out the dead
the dead
piled over the mounds
like tiny cinders of moth wings, and disappeared

A Black Snake
Lives
in the Garden

crawls his long body along the rows
familiarly
his head lifts among the rose bean blooms

he (drinks from the drain
stretches high as corn ears tasseling
and rubs against the tomatoes

his house is the earth
in the storm
he lay quiet as a root buried under

A Day
When the Bare Trees
Are Full of Fluttering

birds have taken over our chicken runs

flocking back against the change
sparlings
to sweep echoing wings
down the unused chimney brick rafters
they flow

beneath weather paper
a colony of usurpers screaming in the barn
and mating pairs
come back from Mexico—as we have come,

deep woods feathers
stained hard as jungle leaves
                       raging the fields
parrot sprays of color:
we sit

   cold in the house
watching their dull efforts
hunting for little left quills to put in their
nests

The Little
Mime

that animals are
using their eyes and ears
rolled in fur

the definite gesture

understood in all
vowel mute, constant
the flesh
moves in the instant
they
       whole
       study our faces, pass
       over us
in a heavy insolence of joy
their   eyes
hold
a compassionate toleration to our

hard
ignorance

Gauguin

from that place, time

I thought of your pictures
women with naked breasts
washing on rocks deep in a
river, banks

where children ran their naked
genitals, turning my head
a white shame

boy
racing a white horse
over a white rock hill
a stripped palm frond
he whipped his horse
over our campfire

black skin ocean of bathers
I hang your round of paintings
the oil
    magazine prints
seeps through the pulpy paper
purples shadow the blues a
startling red, one spot

out of the geometry of sequence
tiles and roofs, a grass-hut
world
I touch the breast you touched
wild naked boy watching with stretched
eyes, an old man with a cane
waits by the same road
as I wait, a rattling many-seater
bus
    comes out of the clearing

In
Arkansas

we drive through the bottoms, old road
packed wash and dirt—
our lights off, the close trees
reach, spreading to our fenders, slowly
we break through the dark areas

watching
water settled rushes to near our car wheels;
we hear wolves howl, a panther
rush (sound in the tree tops, our noise
wakes the birds

wakes the dead woods with our passing

U Quapaw graves. One is buried
low in our own land grove; we never
dug down to see—the thick rocks
spread flat to make his shape
a long arrow
shaft of the wind thrown deep
covered with earth, hollow with roots

we hear them calling against our lights,
when our house lights
stand out against the night like a one
secure shelter; we make our eyes big open places
to see them

we move with a knowledge before their ways
conscious as moving birds of their presence
not still—
we go very slowly and without speed knowing
the dead in the wood
with cold eyes their still graves measure us

The Little
Coati

i
                      when he died body
shuddering in strokes
growled at the fear strange movements running
his brain (in the woods we thought
the striped-back tiger claws
a mouth closed on his throat
                   but
he knew us. lay still as his master slightly
snored; cried out the man's hand waking
to ease down on him

he didn't cry when I held his feet—for pain
the voice low in soft still song-words
they grow to, loving the human

when we buried him
the angel-wings his ears turning stiff
under the fur mouse-ears
we look up /we see his paw lift
suddenly when we walk out or in his
range: his face

the 'most flexible' nose
becoming just firm before in the rain
we could dig his grave

ii
we buried him with flowers
one big red paper an imaginative
mind flower
some hand made without pattern the
firm stem we wound at his feet
rolled in a little ball of the world
coati-mundi coil they sleep in

at his feet we lay
bundles of daisies orange yellow

17

white and stiff whirl petals
centers of the sun
down in the box under the ground

where the mind can't go

iii
facing the east

we put
stones from Mexico
around where the earth had been
dug
                        remembering once
how he stood up a bed of soft
fern holding out his front
feet bounced into their covers

how his paws
went up buffering his nose (a three
monkey clown that could see no evil—
green clover in thick grass pine smell
coming back at last to this house this
yard
                lying in the grass
not cut the big weeds
made shade for his eyes

or on the island river
fort of the flowers
the slope-white gardenias pushing up
over quick-mashed blooms in the coffee
berry grove
                        (under umbrella trees

we put
a black onyx stone over his heart

iv
when he couldn't

                    see anymore
when the eyes began to sink
the end of
that little rooter-tip nose moist
and still black
              moved
as I spoke to him; he couldn't
put a hand to an ear
or cheep or chatter but just
a shiver of knowing
left in the nose

and I sat like god
wanting him to die because
i couldn't help him

v
once through wires of a cage
he attacked a bear
black bear in zoo we gave bread
to, and the bear had the bread

shut up in a cage)
              the coati
climbed high as his head the
bear's head trying to knock
the bread out of his mouth

the big black bear
watched wise as the elephant
child story
having conversation with (a mouse

but the bear of course ate the bread
the world being such as it is he

didn't share it, and the coati

trailed back to the car
where all bread
and round hen's eggs, seeds nuts
jams and
good things of the earth he knew

came from

vi
I sat we didn't cover the body
        when we went out
and dug his grave we knew
he was dead

he didn't seem dead lying there
nothing to be afraid of
once
I felt his forearm above the
paw and a pulse moved

we couldn't see breath
it took some time
before either of us could discern it was
our own pulses
beating against the stillness his stopped
breathing made

we lay the red wool cover light
above him
still for warmth cautious
we didn't want
even then to shut all air off

October
Morning

from the clear fields

waking, half asleep
three black forms
      outside our low windows

a neighbor's cows, black angus
heifers—they looked
in the half-shadow like great
black bears
come out of the forest lairs
  the woods
river range where wolves run
in packs, and single
wild hunts to the edge of
farms

peacefully cropping
their heavy shapes
through the pungent wet grass

when the man passed
going to the low bottoms' fences on his tractor
the dense black beasts
turned
their stubborn heads, uneven minds
turning with the tractor

     fat burdened bodies
hard hooves hitting the still
morning

Honey
it's May

Kiki
        is trailing a mole through the ground
the male coati
lies in the grassy sun
watching for   the postman

                two orange spotted cows
                stand on a slope in the woods' meadow

                two wise jays
                court in the burr grass
                where the long worms mate

                the dog walks
                behind the pregnant whelp
                following the yard trails
                fat with possession

and you work alone in the garden

the black-snake lies
stretched in the tree
eating wild cherries

Honey
it's May

                              (ii
        the big blue cardinal
        flies down from the mimosa
                        across the porch
        feeds in the dog pan

        drinks
        from a chicken trough

        they are not afraid of us
        the birds
        familiar as chimney sweeps
        that sing back of the fire hearth

        a red jay
        sits on wooden arm of the porch swing
        quarrels through the window

        the school of larks
        has taken to the air
        teaching its young to fly
        their wings move

        old as the sound of leaves breaking

        caught in the sudden wind

The Mocking Bird,
his mimic art

lay on the ground
dead grass flutter
earth nest

with morning the wings spread
drooped down like a death shawl
his head fell in mourning

excrement at his feet
'birds die all the time' (yes birds die
natural and human
i thought they died on the wing if i
thought of it
                    proud and pitiful
he held
his last breath under his wing
through the light, all day
we kept him
another morning you couldn't see that
he was dead, he stood

like a little performer
who knows his own secrets
                    singer, lark of the air

as though
his song took off suddenly
hurled to the ground
under the feathers, his own sleep

Wolves

come up to the pond
and take a drink of water

run across fence line
sit on the bank
                and cry

they cry
sitting above the moccasin holes
under the dead tree
that lightning struck

it is winter—
chickens in the barn black
feathers fat like crows
pole legs stuck up on the roost

one round as a bird
high on the sweet gum

rabbits burrowed deep below
thick berry vines sticker-brush
and dogs sleeping

wolves
eyes open as stars
                bellies lank
stick up their wet noses

crying to the empty sky and earth

haunched on the still pond bank
lapping up drinks of water

Heavy
with Winter

burrowed down here
out of moon burn

all shut over
from that

fertile rare sun
where
sleep-warm seeds

wake

in self
and all this bitterness

        breaks

           hard
           in unabsorbent

                still

           in our
           plant time

           and the earth
           cakes dry

           without water
           soaked to the hull

           of patterned days

                waiting

Hunters
in the Snow

i
a covey of quail, frost-feeding

      in the just-turned yard grass
come up to the house rove, they walk
alert the high breast in air
runner-walkers, breaking from a field fence
uncut stalks cover their ways

as we came through the young corn in July
we frightened them
tiny bulb feathers
a wind of acorns getting out of the rows; now
bright fruit stalks cropping on active legs
their quick heads

lift in crests of color, the male, the old male
watching
is he the same my father tamed—nested
with a hen, raised with chickens
but that was years past;
how long does a wise quail live on seed?
long as our love

cold in the snow (the warm earth
  in crisp heaves of light, they move
we must repair the barn, winter is coming
grind the sprouted grain and seed—on flows of
loneliness and ice
sun-brakes their shadows come in on us
whistles of keenness, through a shrill wind
they clothe us in feathers

flames racing in the near-flame
soft under-green stubble, come in from
woods ways; they throw
their bright flames
against the stacked brush we never burned
against the clearing

ii
yellow-breasted larks flown south in November

edge of woods
in river bottoms of timber, still cows
graze the fence lines
they wake us with their heavy bawls calling
to summer

and over the turned cold grass
the larks, in sudden morning a warm sun
settles
lift; they flurry to posts, a bare limb
red-bud is full of them
the big pine we almost burned one year
is thick with new needles; its low branches
cut, it stands
high over us a flame of green on flames of
other green, the still woods

deep in—droves of wolves and old wolf lairs
we wait the return of driven down bodies
the larks
sing

they sing of the gulf and palm ways
they sing of north oaks and where they came from

iii
soon we'll have the earth creatures, moving down

the drains
crying at night, droves
lonely ones with lonely whines, lonely in their hunts
it's a pleasure to drive to town through the leaves

i stay in spring looking forward to a garden, then
a change comes
                    i dream of wild ways
and there is
something about the 'wild ways' that comes to us
the strangeness. a day just feeling of
winter, frost on the grass (killing to most things
still some underneath green
. . . and the pines

when i went out to the shed house
yesterday
sparrows were building flock shelters
burrowing under the weather paper
they flew, fluttering against tin eaves their
sounds warm
back with us. come out of their summer tree-
cool air nests
settling in little family hovels
against the vine and wall shrub that cover
the hearth place. they slither
under barn rafters where we work and hide
they will cry
with the wolves all through the snow
gay and in clusters

the Old Woman Who Never Dies, the indians called
her, she who makes the crops grow
sending messages
by even the birds that passed; they shot up, arrows of
stars, their wings floating in sunlight

Heaved
from the Earth

after the tornado, a dead moccasin
nailed to the pole
boards scattered across a pasture

lying fierce crosses
jagged in mud

had flung itself
nail and wood
the square-head animal
hurled also in air

or as it raced in weeds
)water flowing, water falling
impaled
      both the snake and timber
went flying through with wind

coiled, made a coil (they do
immediately from danger or when hurt
and died in a coil
bit itself
in pain of its own defense the poison

          birds
          hurled into yard
          fences
          one with feet tangled gripping
          the open wire, a big Jay

struggling from the water
throwing its fanged head
high at the lightning, silent
in all that thunder

to die by its own mouth
pushing the fire thorns in

The Red-brown
Spider

reflecting light
pushes her egg bag feeling
over grass, silk shadows
her legs

rolled into leaf webs, a web
of parchment down
she rolls to a hollow about the
distended bulb, dangles
from string

spit glue, dew fiber
throws her long rope out
and swings a cradle
from tree limb

her body is covered with fuzz
when she feels herself to the ground
her body
is covered with legs
light-lifted, light-shadowed
hundreds
a hundred little gauze weavers

tumble over her
threads of air creatures, air feelers
huddle on her back
throw, hurling their

nets of hair into green leaves

Fall Surprise Lilies
Spring Up

          in a clump after the mowing
their sap-light feelers
feeling for leafless light

burst in high air-bed of petals
red hands
red as blood
a blanket of blood blown from the stems
stands

suspended against the fence line
grown from root bulbs
glass wires
dangling each gauze with yellow seed-
pollen
out of the spangles drooping
the moths

tiny wings and larger wings
fly and flutter and sit down in the light
they are soft as wings
they are soft as wings in the flowers
come from the grass

sleeping under grass leaves
they invade the meadow of petals

Flood Rain,
Wind

washing the plowed earth raw
you ran from it
at last
sat in the dark confusion of water

plants wouldn't grow

then even in storm
against the deep flare cuts
a red sun
(ball of fire
hurled up from what we thought was
night
hung there
caught in a mesh of lightning

in back of us
a cleared reflection
     fierce over trees, tops
bent holding the wind thrown
hard with color

we traced in our hands
where the bow fell

To My Father
in the
New House

from poems of Dickinson's Nursing Home, 1968–69

he walked over the earth-tile floors
winter was coming
uniformity of heat
                    he missed
the back screen porch his old place
the pump the well his cows his chickens
filling the water trough

go out snow on the ground break
skating layer of ice
                        hens in the
tall hackberry sullen limbs night
frost-feathers shut up in sheds under
roosting poles, a tree

the way crest of the
walnut reached high throwing down
a bed of green balls rolling
gum-stain hulls
his white horse standing under its arches

fire, a round of logs in hearth and
lamp light /going to minnow pond
wading with throw net in that
dark water

under the quiet asbestos shingles
                        you didn't wake
rain all-wood walls that seeped with
moisture, the boards got wet
sleet banked his shallow window cuts and
storm threw shadows the lightning
ran over ridge beams

The Tiny
Baby Lizard

wiggling head-first from the egg
down in a burrow
hole made hard and soft in the dirt, the wise
lizard creature mother
hatching her eggs

the belly of her body
warm he runs over the still startling color
moving head, reaching down
drapes over her neck between legs curls
a long curl string
in the coiled curve of her flesh, the body

lying in the dark
her alert calmed head, not darting
not slithering as they do in the open rushed
from fear, weed ways and rock ways

he learns first the quiver quiet
flesh-way
earth-instinct circumference
he eats from her mouth

From the
Chamberino House:
New Mexico

we woke, at first we thought it was air suction the
cotton gin: cotton yet small in the fields, a
train—

looking out over the lettuce rows
wet with irrigation
the sprawling flat ranges of plant and cultivated
area between the mountains, past the river
we sat on the door steps
birds

flying from the pass
screamed in the darkness
all the houses were asleep; two cars
came with distant lights following a distant
road

the steady high-air sound that a rocket makes
and we wondered
what 'they' were making at White Sands, if
the works blew up
a tree, against a plastic window
looked for a moment like a pillar of smoke: anything

off, over, against the skyline
of sand and white shape and ghouls that walked the
meadow-ways. the night before, congress
was arguing over what to do with
de-moded nerve gas, at last

we got in the car to go some place, telephone, call
town, to drive and see a dead world wake—the
gas
was seeping down
you smelled it full in the road
and we sat until morning, still in the house again
waiting for the strange sun to come up; even the animals
came inside with us

All Day
the Big Monarchs
Fly

their orange bleak-edge fans
blown by the wind, settling in
wet grass
we see only their wings

each one
going the same direction, south and
west—
pushed by the cold, pulled
by the equator, they sail

over the roads, above the highways
droop with the quickness of rain
they are like leaves
lifting from the windshield

like leaves
falling to the ground, being hurled
they roll
through air currents, wisps of air
little papery feathers

that the hand could melt; big soft flakes
near to snow, the light
shines through each wing
suddenly

Coming Back
Through the Night,
Mountains

Indian ridges
huddles of yellow-fur sheep, flares
camp-watchers with their
wood fires against the cold

wind blows at our windows

a house of shattered glass, the
shattering glass
spreads before our floodbeams
stiff stars
hanging suspended Christmas tree bulbs
high among the peaks, spare
trees

driving into the past
when the road lifts
a new old people are filling the woods
                    —without change
they wear sheep's wool
their clothes are the color of sheep

their minds move quiet as sheep
before their campfires
their faces burn with
fires burning, in their hands
stones are being gathered; they
hold the stones not hurling them at our
silent windows

the dark covers them

In the Garden

a brown-breasted
flyer, the female
fell over the wall
through the air's
white radiance

she lay
heaped with her hurt bill
broken, and
the futile tongue
loose to suction
the fire-need gone

she could die there,
in earth rest
under trees
where her mates sang

and they flew down;
she tore
her loose wing
joints out
against the rock-shock
into the leaf
wall shade
as they cried in light, above her

The Valley
of San Miguel

from *The Valley of San Miguel*

i
the black giant
stalks on four legs up and through the
drain ditches, races
the still fields rows of round-head
lettuce

the old land-owner, hound of the valley
without involvement
bellows his rules of the lettuce-
ways

he is like a stiff bud pecan
with all leaves shook off
he is a wilting sprout, the mesquite
cleaned of its beans
blooms

in its own black wholeness

ii
the first night
he sat with us at table 'this
is my land' he said
                    not in words
we left him locked in his own
wonder

how silent the fields are
growing food

poems
of cold

the big mountain (stretched

sprawled out its muscles
but when i opened the camera
from its rock shell
            the bending earth
rolled hard and austere, they stood
before us

Painter
Crayon 1

i
the low-circle SUN
through the burned wood
lies like a blown coal

against the peeling white-hull conifers

    sets a feeble blaze
flickering into the chill ash
circumference

ii
sage leaf bushes
a sprinkle of peppermint
purple and broken-apart

seed spools
under-fringed with smell

the wild rose
petals of crisp cups
breaks in wilting fragment-
shatters
its pollen floe
floats on the melted rivers

iii
quills
like spurs of wheat
the moving thistle puff
wheeled in fur-fuzz
soft as hatched bird
feathers

the cotton that flutes
from tree blossom buds

birds their bills full
peck out the drifting fine-thread
mats, they hover down
shaking them damp from the current
to build weaving above the thawed bank
cones sweet with

breaking quill and
their hovered young

Rain Sleets
Flat

bending down the huddle sprout grass
lights in puddles between the grass spindles
settles
washing crevices dense into
the bank of graves

the earth is covered with clods and rock
caked over

above
habitat high on the mountain
like some strange shell blown there, thrown
dripping
the cave
its bare opening pours gulped with watery sand

the dead
lie in their brief houses
there is nothing to wake them
they are safe from the wolves

North from
Tanyana

these are the woman mountains

the without shame cold

the sun has circled around her breasts
and heated her pelvis
she sprawls
face up, stomach heaved full and loaded
the legs braced
thighs and knees holding in their long wait (belly
flat
        a child's game of statue whirled
in light another
thrown under the pelvis
an arm from the chest is falling down
the upper arm held above, into
the clean spaces of air
lifts a breast softly

waiting for what giant who will take her

low trees brush up the sides of her legs
spread unprotected
the winds and the great thaws to ravish her
caribou bite at her nipples
wolves rove down from the thick edges of gravity
stand, in the defenseless waste
singular range
shapes on the high moors of silence
chains of silver snow against the throat

the woman abandon mountains
the frame-pierced cold
their buttocks and faces are turned sidewards as in
sleep

an avalanche of women
hurled from the peaks of winter, they lift toward
        the long awaited
from still valleys (lovers
the turf shines like green silk
over the young flesh of their shoulders

men riding down on golden horses
out of the snow

the sun has taken over all the pastures

young moose hide in the willow clumps
the sun is grazing on the open hills

the thick grass is fresh laid-out in patches
moves as light is moved
like a slaughter of hides
stretched clean for the tanning, as though
some certainty of hand had placed them

Mass
of the Flowers

i
its rock-brown
           pollen tassel
the diamond willow
scorches the bush-brush timber
july

the red spindle flower
that makes, winding
shaking in wind
startled spindles when the brief forms fall
copper-rock flowers
           breaks of fall weeds
their dried pulp milk joints
brittle as castor leaf
smoke up in live dust

sage
that burns absorbed with purple
fields in rows a heather of wild sage
yellows, and whole blues

slopes vivid as
barn paint
annuals of leaf among the evergreen

ii
yellow moss fir
near over the
               ranges
heat in the ground
seeps up
its even-fluid fire

iii
bark log rivers

a tundra of grass hay
beyond piled rock fences

death (is quiet
as a log rotting in water
its roots
melting with ice heap, a log roll
of dead limbs budding

below a summer field of wild deer
pawing their hooves
bedded in the bent down snow pulp
close fungus
    they will bite off the first stems

blown wing-sparrow leaves set flying
into the narrow grass banks
small bodies
their feelers drift balanced
in summer draw

iv
fingers
soft as light, measuring
to thin shafts
from the sterile lye mountains

bear-man tracks
straddling the heaped slowly shifting
woods

Plateaus

i
above the ledges of red clay, breaking
banks
a hurl perpendicular flat of
green slab stone

peaks of blanched lime-salt at night
the alkali salt
slush-gummed
quick and livid in shale, their projection
a dehydrate steam

in the lean ash trembling trees
   veins
    of cobalt loom on the settled edges

a flint-struck light
flames
through the forest

ii
the wind bleaks sad snow
across the tundra
it frosts in scattered melt
drops
turns liquid on
    the held-heat stones

the wind
sleets a blue rain of snow
cold over the flat hill elevation
the tundra rolls swelled thick with gathered
shapes
toward the blister peak
summits

iii
a bird

feathered with down
under feathers of
rain

against the blue cloud
ravine caverns
a hole in the cloud
sifts in ice

   the trembling mountain
holds
above the wind

drifts of intermittent
light

iv
the earth builds
from marrow of bone
bone-marrow

the sweet heart-willow
with its heart that is eaten black
stone-centered
wings of arrow tips
held in sulphur fire

the earth turns to sand
its dug-out marrow
makes chalk torsos, a spread
of bones
made hard

fibrous
and steady with color

Painter
Crayon 2

the SNOW

balances the forests
levels into mountains

tarnishes
the tall strip trees and bark
a fluttering metal

over stiff high stalks
where once hung leaves
green

limbs
coming up from fragile stems
like long-fall hair
straightening in the wind

the fields
lie dead, thrown with big
hand-full clusters of roses
smothered in grass

banking the root woods
high the rain-wet decaying
branches
broken up and twisted, set
pungent
in this yet summer frost

        the blue whale
        sperms
        a blue iodine
        that stills
            into the water

Mountains

the women dream of
snake and lizard
they sleep with black warriors

the ridges spread
like weeping dinosaurs
long bone
skeletons
above their green blankets

warped bones
struck up white in cold and filled with
skeletons of women
a woman flung her hair out weeping
the great still female form the shoulders
haunched down
moves us—
covering her hard mature breasts
the mountain piled dead with
war arrows
set clean with weeping

women abandoned
left to their keeping
alone, hovered over with loneliness
their backs held thrown (without claim

graves among aloes and iris
graves among willows

like left old men
carving out intricate snake heads of war—
washing in the rain
quiet a cemetery of great sad peaks
cemetery of dinosaur and snakes that
crawl, turtle heads

the snake head where there is no snake
pyramids
dripping their slaughter
with forgotten blood

filtered with the dead, weeping with anger

Horses
of the Moor

galloping down the cold range places

white horses
that walked in the garden
under the white husk
almond trees

        a guitar player
        filled the shadows
        with reflections

the hand of the guitar player
moves a green reflection on the wall
the sun
places yellow on the hills
lamps on the wall

women in lines like flower pots
wicks of lamps against the stones
a leaf,
a white horse under the black and yellow orange trees

horse manes
horses in the dust
horse feet slipping on the purple rock-mud
sediment of these absorbent rivers

The Indian End
of the Summer

i
copper beaches
slow with ice

glacier slate
crushed up
a startling blue
rainbow rinse

rust in silver birch trunks
        glistening in tops of trees
a limestone of beech and white pine
shaling down
the protected hills

   reflections of ore in the air
beyond the trees
the extreme limits of fire

ii
behind them
light like fire the Indians made
Indians with pitch lanterns
holding up the pitch of their lanterns
a big cat's eyes
its wild slither
a tormented panther-dark pushed full and high
by the yellow panther glow

Indian muscles
        beat against the tendon flesh
their long flung-thin arms
long stretched through the skin

iii
blood on the mountain

dragged up
after the riders

crusted snow

The Volcano Rocks
Wear Penitent Black

i
down their crater sides
drain
with dregs of

great hawks and eagles
floating and flapping

clay tombs with grass covers
bones
of the harvested earth
bodies laid near one another
in tracks of congealed fire ice
phosphorous approaching the winter-
white glow, a range of radium

fierce as firefly tails
chips in snakes of light, melt
from
formations of stone

ii
under the wheeling hawks
the sacrilege
singular empty black vault open to the
sky

a black wood cross
where once a meadow was
plains above the naked stripped land
the mutiliated
an above-spread graphite shelf
bare and precipitous

in the dark woods' leaves
the dense shade cast by foliage

vegetation matted together
ferns and mosses, the hawks
suspend their wings

wavering body-nests
that cross through the cold north rain

the rocks drape penitent black their
heaps of great bent bows
the sun has shot through them
its last bright wedges

a rove of black wolves
wander lost in the meadows

A Dream
in Cold

the sun eyed fire-macaw sits in a white tree
at corner of the universe

                                                          (i

      north is the horizon
      south lies heat
      past the horizon's rim the warm inland bay
      a bird with white wings
      sleeps
      the rivers of melting water
      never wake her
      she sleeps and dreams

      'but i am a bird whose song is cold'

      carved bone the sun rims over
      an all night long of waking
      splintering with sticks like strokes of fire
      burns and dazzles
      and shoots its high shafts into the drawn
      bows of violet
      pointed arrows, the frozen wings

                    'i am a bird
                      whose dream is of heat
                      who sings of the cold'

down the blue-curved mountain glacier
white bear fur
swallows under the fish-hut eaves fish nets
                fragile at still windows
fish scales of shimmer ice
falling from ledge to ledge, sails
that plunge circling
surrounded with frozen islands of water

hawkweed and birds—
melting down the blue-cloud mountains
they bring with them
                      bells
                      the spear bone
and candles from bee's wax

the men hunt for the feather
from the white bird for their arrows

over drift peaks the wind-blown rain

                                                (ii
                                        'a white bird flying low
                                        against the white ground'
                                        (the snow

            moves cold above the tundra
            its mist heavied up
               in the air suspended

            on tipped flint
            split-resounding boulders
            the thunder
            beyond the long flat frozen roll
            wolves
            the white bear that lapped in cavern falls
            pointed,
            the swift rain cuts through the sky
            from settled natural pyramids of space

            drawn from the low ice-free ridges
            of grass land

            white and glistening
                            the full-tip woodline
            warm lateral valleys
            a jungle of sudden creepers
            and fawn-hair aspen

            leaving the cave by starlight
            a monster of fallen avalanche
            smokes over, scented and sulled
            brief
            the solid melt turns

            splendidly down a wild gorge opening of
            cliffs

            serpents crawling through the dark
            the living
            have broken into the graves and pulled the dead about

falling like fluffs of stars
a few flakes of
               grass stems and
lark feathers
flocks of simple herd feeding next to
where the sun was
surrounded by fields of winter

it was growing dark
no lamps were allowed
stones hurling plunged into the deep side gullies
the white bird
high on the furtherest boulder

has drawn his shot wings

Painter
Crayon 3

i
as going north
the slow abandon
death of the flowers
shallow in rain

the first death
settles
                from the snow
on the inner-EARTH

ii
the white bear
growls from his cave
isolated
among the glacier plateaus

dips his fur in blue
through frosted blocks of ice
a wallow of air-change
moves on the lake, surging

up its banks

iii
leaf-spread drops under a tree
a hail of evidence
dripping on wide leaves

weighing down pellets of hail
against the chill-set jungle

a hover of soft cumuli
clouds
and butterfly moths
                with agate tip wings

iv
snow leaves

blow over the tundra
carved figures and bodies in
leaf prints
drift
dip into animal pasture dens
tracks that wander the
rove chill hills

ember whirls of rock crystal
in masses of crystal
brood in the sleet
cylinders held close they quiver sound

globes frozen like winged seeds
blowing

a glass light
beyond the green-light, close
place we see in

From Painted
Grave-houses

the rain sags, narrows the sappy boards
seeps a bog wash under holes
where the lone wolves crawl
they gnaw the riddled hot-swell meat

in a dead heather of plants
the sunk-in skeletons (that lay
skulls strung on a rope of bark
they lie on their backs
heads at last ease turned sidewards
regarding down

at their long trunks with their huge eyes
having left them

flat grave land
sifted up by water
a piled up heap of willow bark, the heart
seeped through

Sacrifice to Sound:
the Morning

blue and wild, a mist
of separation

    barren land reefs
far-held patches of sky and earth
rising on
weights of watery-rots of ice
like a crusted filter vapor, warped

the tears of the 'land of shadows'
not desolate

men huddled in fur blankets
repairing their spears
the eider ducks are far out on the bay
the people make fish lines

the people are no longer living in tents
caves of ice
they sit with moss in stone lamps
braiding sinew, their thick black braids of
hair
they go toward the shadows
like seals
they make faint breathing sounds

fogs of light and
flying glass
on tails of living green, a reef of extravagant blue
the air forced down
    a covey of small boats pulled to the bank
moved by the wind
held fast with posts

blown heavy to the packed ground

washed up from the holes in the sea

breathing, the fallen blizzard packs
spread fluid
without pulse or muscle, easy
as flung feathers

under the yellow sheets, cracks laid bare
in flow rush
close-grown reflections

the earth's light
goes out above the mountains
the earth's voice
lies buried under the fall of water
the earth-heart
is entirely covered

> trees behind the perpetual
> glaze
> a vertical darkness
> make reverse lakes in the sky
> re-make, and change

The Arctic
Thaw

in the first days of the heavy north melt

no shadow, no vegetation

up and down the ice glades
a constant shower of bright crystal
the air is a hail of star ice
not heard,
north of the trees
snow left in moving tops the spear-shaft
pinewood
upright slabs fallen (in cliffs of flight

between the low cover, lost
the sun glassy
cold through a cut cold stands
like a shelf frosted and smokeless

shifting gales of fine as sand
swollen dunes
dust, source of the wind blown under
beating down over the still hooves of storm

       the body could only lie on its back
       the hands are folded over the nipples

a first huge fish
washed away from the early places
disappears in the rush under rock, a part
of sediment
naked between the scattered clay the uncut
purity, fallen with stones

dead turf, limbs
quick spindling up bare in a marsh of water
cells in fluid stain moveable and
upright they pour
with the long withered and burned
glassed-over surfaces

on treeless oceans of ice

without context, image
monsters of the slide sheet and
rising thaw
submerge
a hard and sterile unity
on the effervescent

land
a wind-drive boat
pulls with the wind
under the full spray
melt

flinging long
    pulse heave strokes
a wheel road
high among and washed to the stars

under the earth, women in earth

their tears

about the horizon, for night

the sun in lit large candles
molded from wax

vaulted in waving lines
clumsily built
clotted with animal blood

nearer, direct
riding over the low pass
a chapel with small bells
beating ornaments of bone and copper

that break in pieces from the scaled difference
quick in summer
pressed back sound, the motionless scabs of
thin white flakes

a melt-down from
        tumble bells of clover
surrounds the fields, glistening
goat horns hung silent on the walls
an infinity of fragments

                the earth
                abstract from heat
                dreams singing with cold
                impersonal
                detached
                isolate, the wings burn
in their steady lay cold

Through Fields
of Fog
and Trembling Winds

the bird's dream is yellow grass
fisher lights
leaves that scatter their great blob paint
north barns
filled with sulphur grass

stones blue as powder sapphire

a damask on crupper of red mane horses
the sun unwinds
high thrown down to the single line of poles
burnt half way up in a desert of frost
the hills spread out
open to the rain

at woodline
above the slate bark woods
trees growing up out of cloud areas
balanced trepid in moisture
vapor frothed heavy in their branches higher now
than any snow
from the great height of its
precipitous sides
      drainage out of the coast-pass wall
at low water
glooms in the forests
                    washed away in places

leaking mud
sluices decaying to flats,
smoking in the wind
growing up from flood stage
moss limbs and crisp bark with yellowing leaves

                    the rebellious
                    will of the mind

cold in its nest
the ornamental head
   bird on a pole above the grave mounds
rock mouth gaping air
appears
similar to those forms south (the hot snake
its feathers stiff

still as the crayon, watching

a note about the author

besmilr brigham (who is part Choctaw) was born Bess
Miller in Pace, Mississippi. She studied writing in the
fifties at the New School for Social Research. She and
her husband, Roy Brigham, have lived in Oklahoma,
Texas, France, Nicaragua, Alaska, Canada, and Mexico,
and are now in Arkansas. Mrs. Brigham has been
published in *The Atlantic Monthly, Harper's Bazaar,*
and various small literary magazines.

a note on the type

The text of this book was set in Medallion, the film version
of Melior, a typeface designed by Hermann Zapf and
issued in 1952. Born in Nürnberg, Germany, in 1918,
Zapf has been a strong influence in printing since 1939.
Melior, like Times Roman, another popular twentieth-
century typeface, was created specifically for use in a
newspaper. With this functional end in mind, Zapf
nonetheless chose to base the proportions of its letterforms
on those of the Golden Section. The result is a typeface
of unusual strength and surpassing sublety.

Composed by Westcott & Thomson, Inc., Philadelphia,
Pennsylvania, and Typographic Innovations, Inc., New
York. Printed and bound by Kingsport Press, Inc.,
Kingsport, Tennessee. Typography and binding design by
Betty Anderson.